# How to get the most out of this coloring book

## Relax

This book is designed to help you
relieve stress,jumpstart your imagination,
relax,get motivated,alleviate frustration,
and help you have fun if you let it.

The key here is you have to let it.
So just color! Don't worry about creating a perfect
piece of art, don't worry about coloring inside
the lines, and if you need to, scribble all over
the picture completely.

## Color

If you are going to color with maarker or paint,
please take the time to cut out the page that
will prevent the color from bleeding through to
the next design.I recommend micro markers or
colored pencils for the intricate designs.

## Discover

Think about what made you want to color
today? Was it stress? Did you need inspiration?
What colors did you use? How where you feeling?
Whether, you learn from you coloring experience
or not, have fun!

## Enjoy!

Use the dotted lines to cut out your favorites to
hang on the wall.

Cut along the dotted line and use this page to place behind the page you are coloring on to prevent color from bleeding through.

If you are using markers a piece of cardboard or heavier piece of paper may work better.

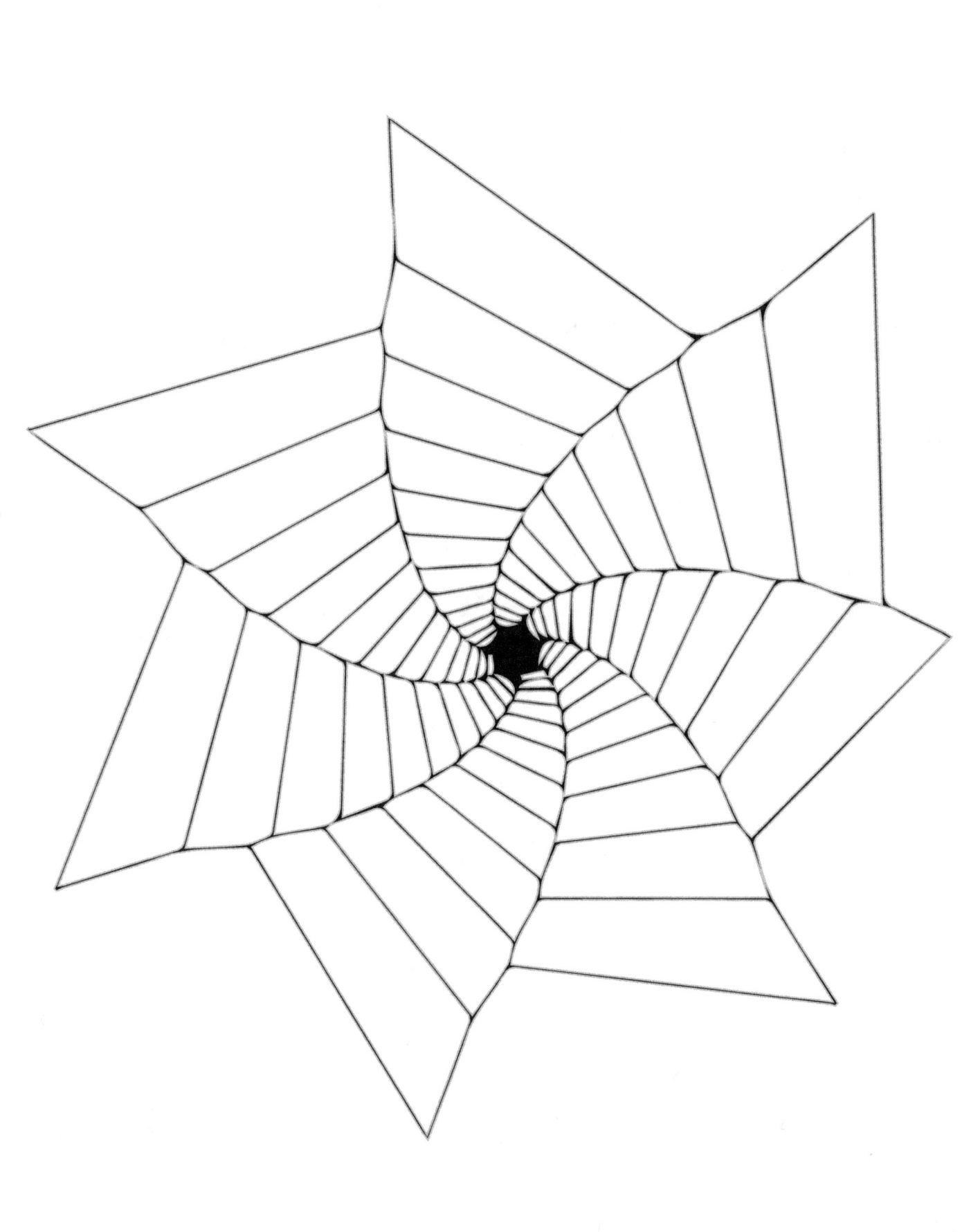

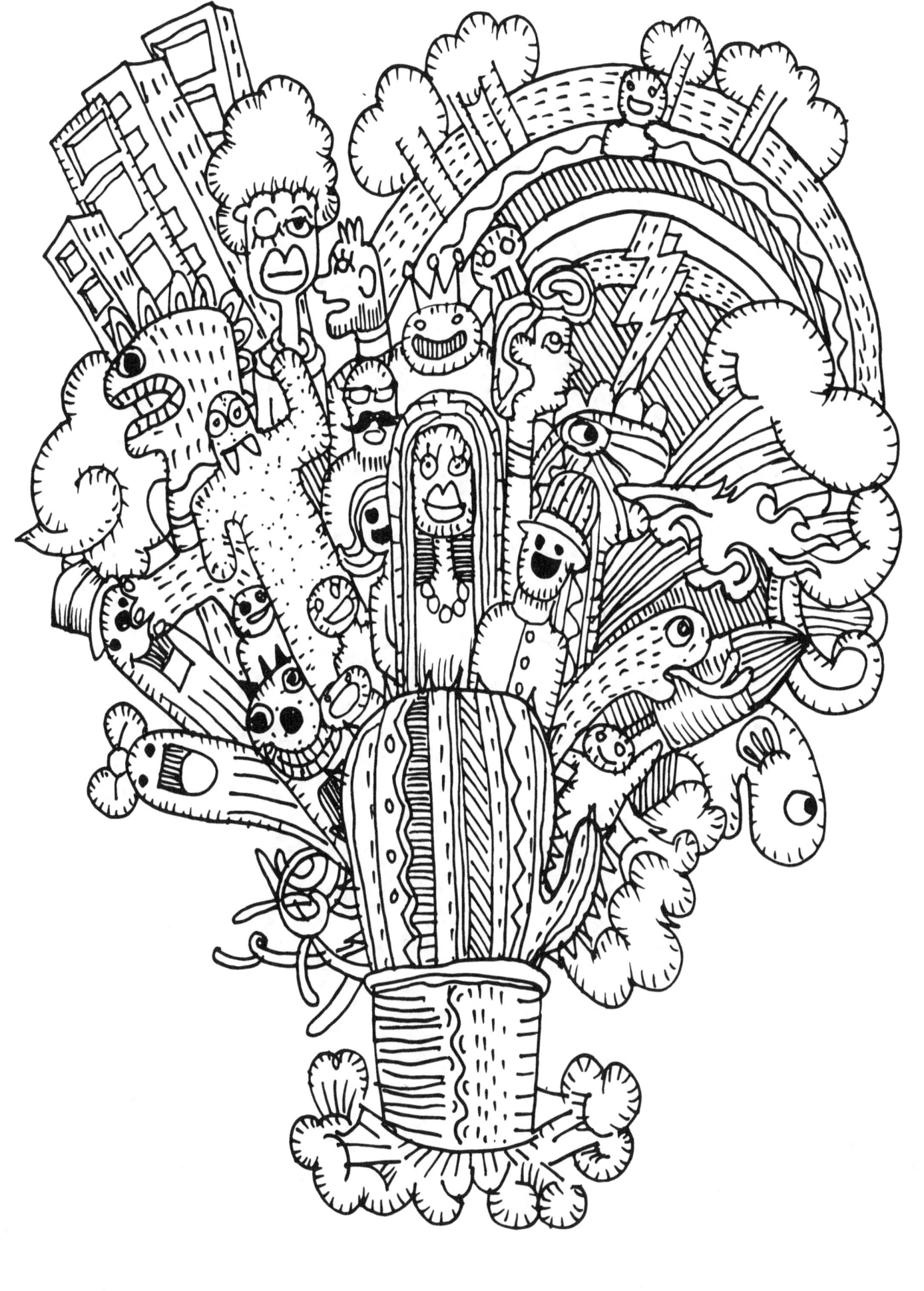

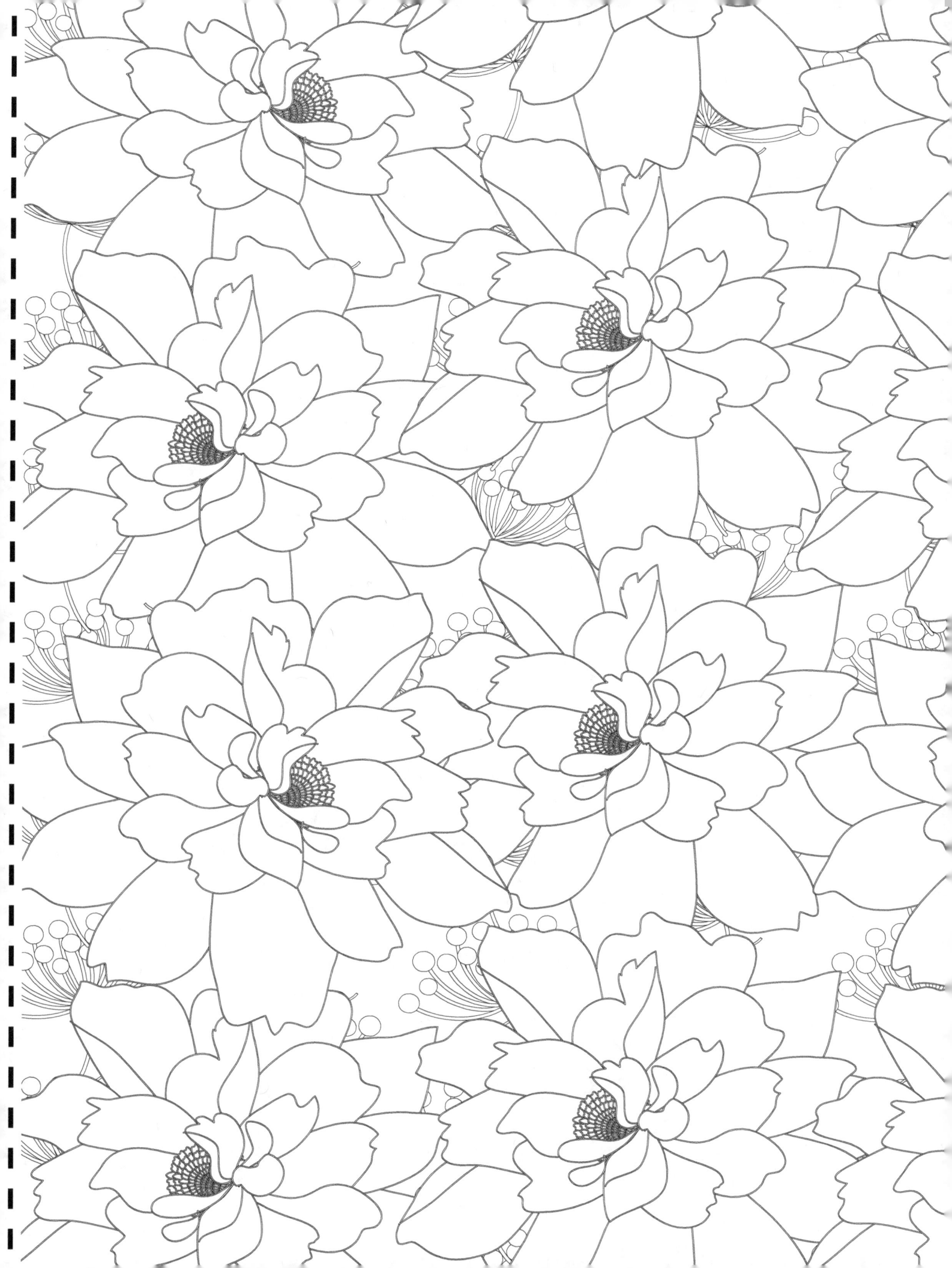

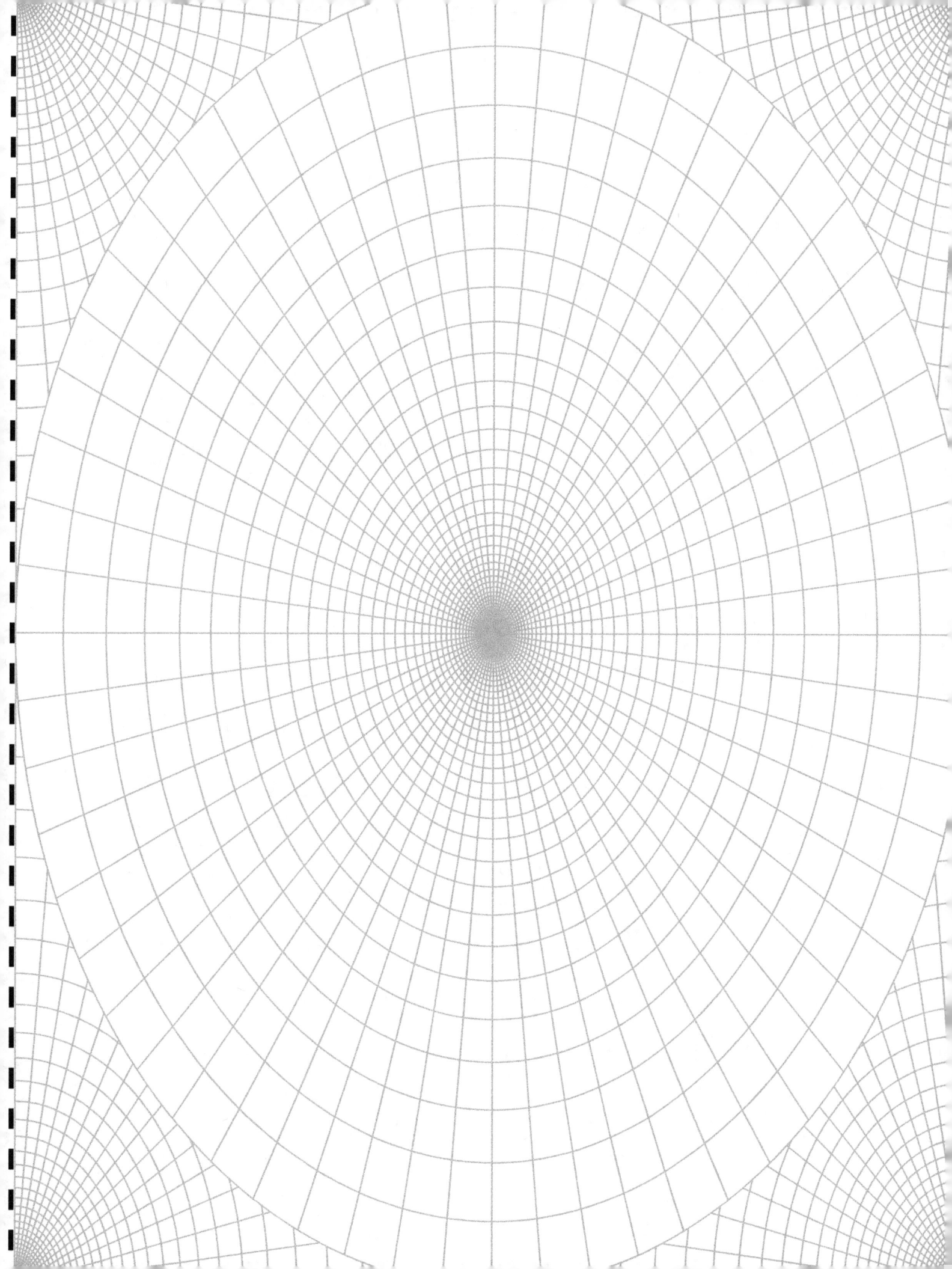

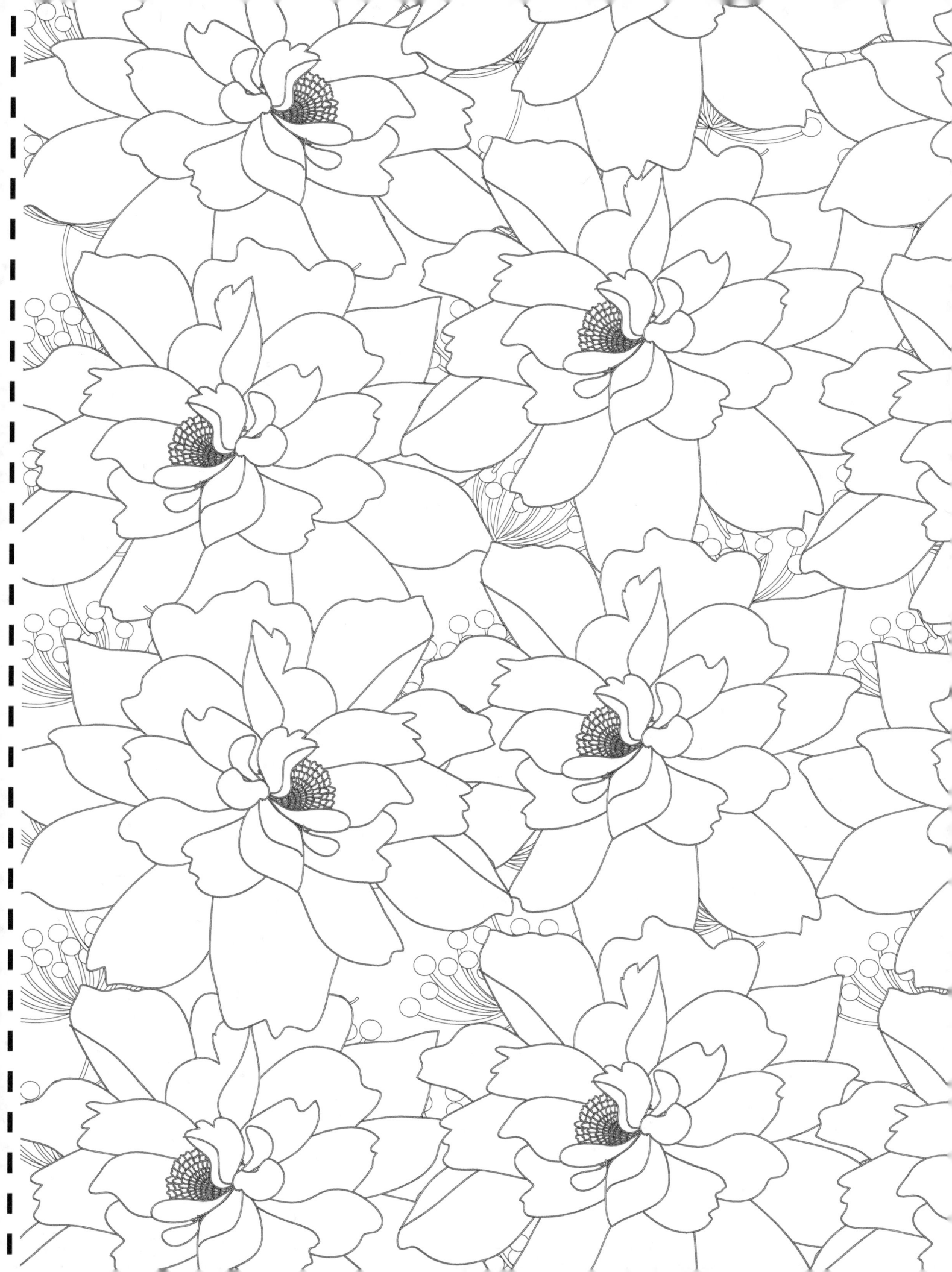

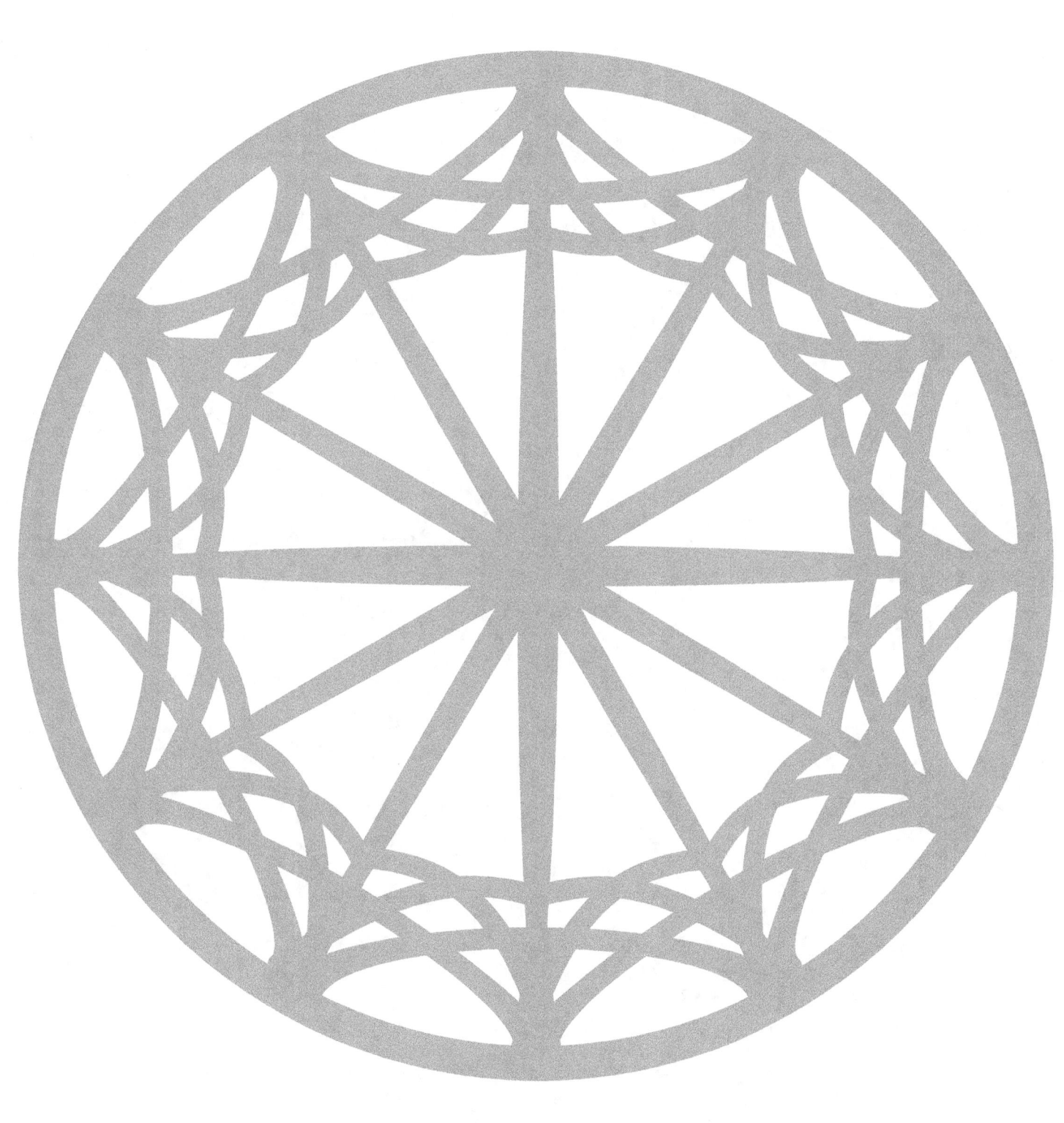

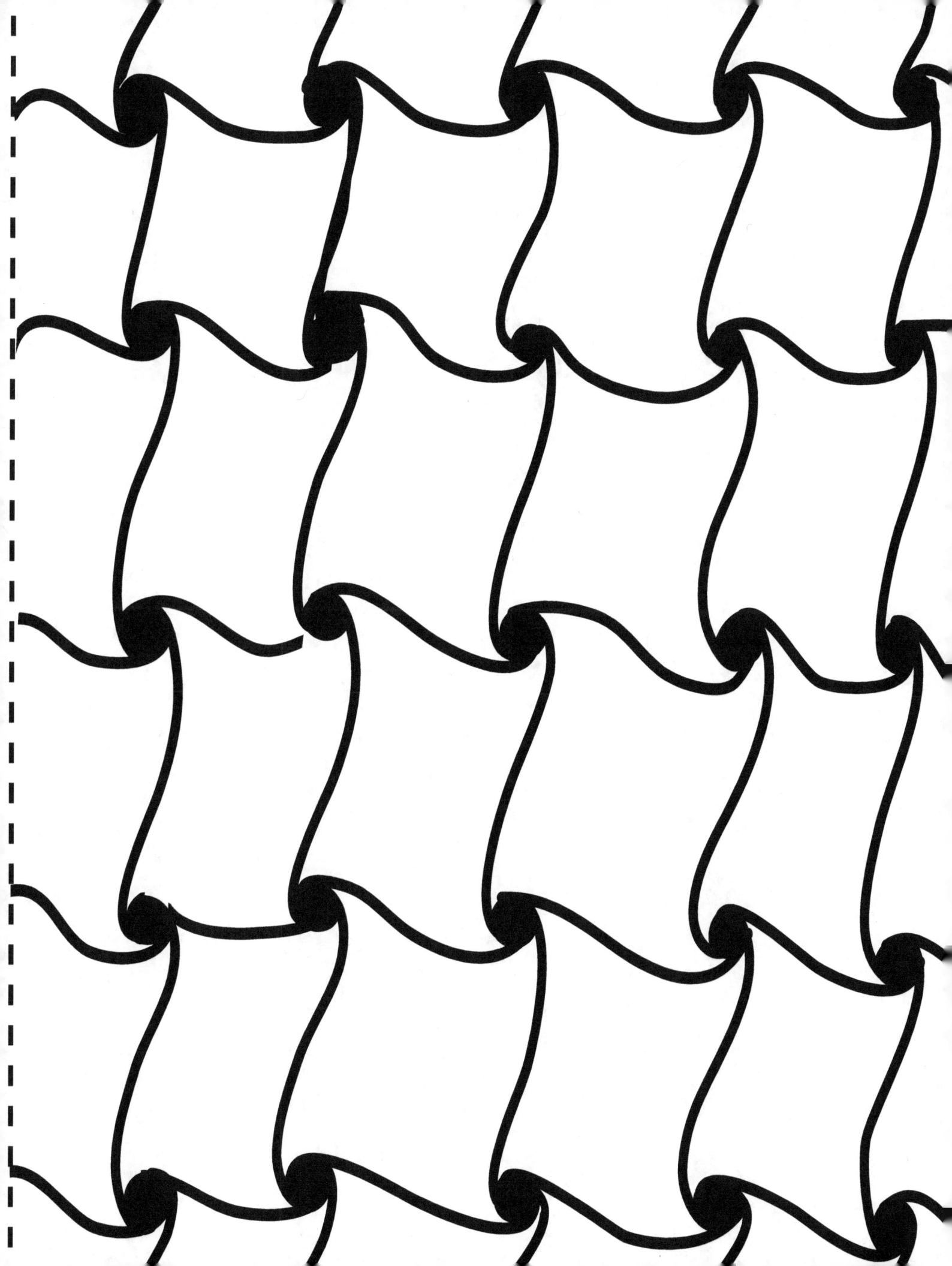

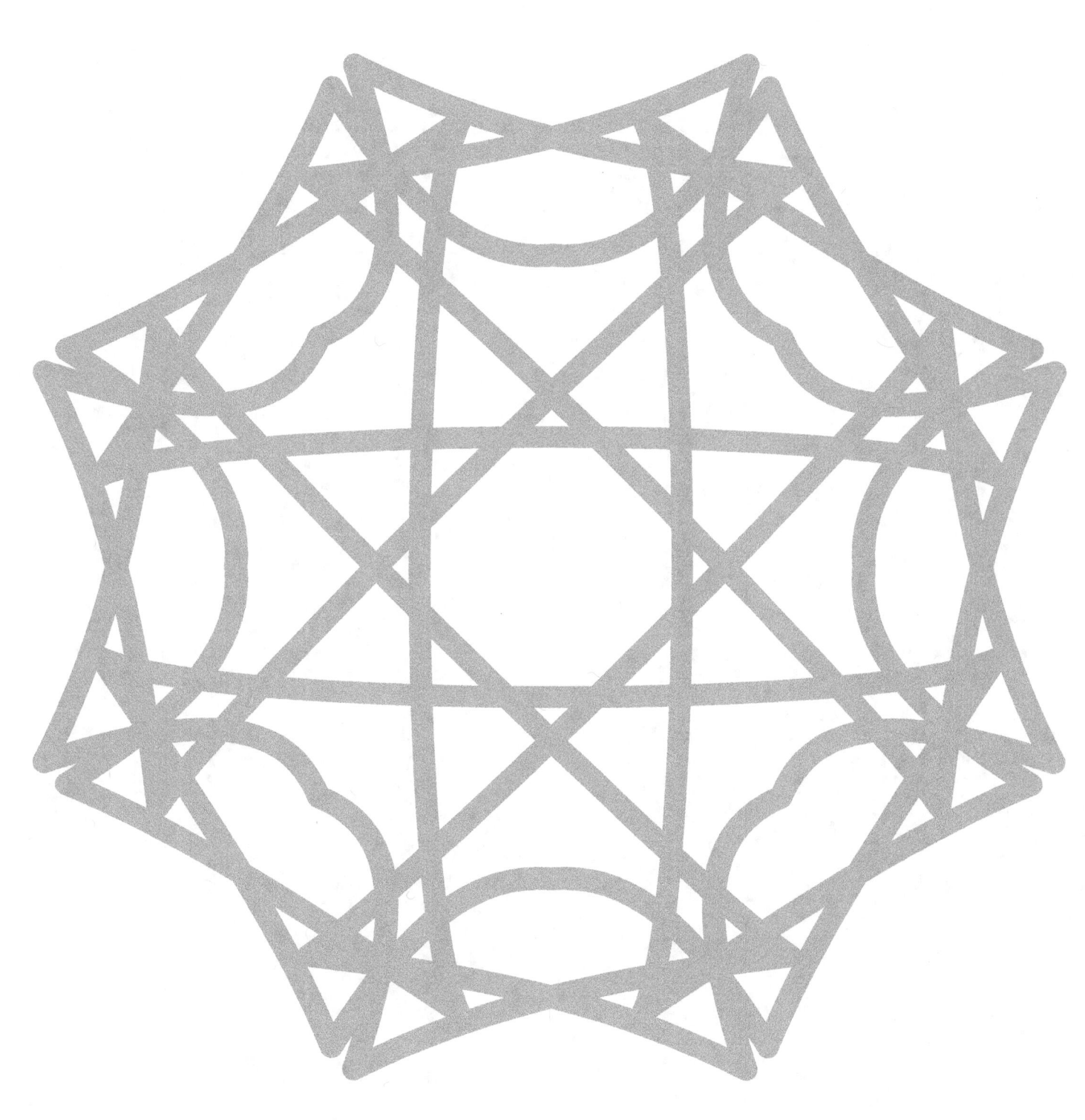

Thank you, for your purchase.

I hope this book has helped you
relax, get inspired, and have fun.